ATOMIC

GHOSTS

MARC TYLER NOBLEMAN

Raintree
Chicago, Illinois

Published by Raintree,
A division of Reed Elsevier, Inc.
Chicago, Illinois

Customer Service 888-454-2279

Visit our website at www.raintreelibrary.com

Printed in China by WKT

11 10 09 08 07
10 9 8 7 6 5 4 3 2 1

Library of Congress Cataloging-in-Publication Data

Nobleman, Marc Tyler.
Ghosts / Marc Tyler Nobleman.
p. cm. -- (Atomic)
Includes bibliographical references and index.
ISBN 1-4109-2523-4 (library binding-hardcover) -- ISBN 1-4109-2528-5 (pbk.)
1. Ghosts--Juvenile literature. I. Title. II. Atomic (Chicago, Ill.)
BF1461.N63 2006
133.1--dc22

2006004043

13 digit ISBNs:
978-1-4109-2523-7 (hardcover)
978-1-4109-2528-2 (paperback)

Acknowledgments

The author and publishers are grateful to the following for permission to reproduce copyright material: Corbis pp. **6** (Benjamin Rondel), **26** (Bettmann), **17** (Catherine Karnow), **13** (Hulton-Deutsch Collection); Getty Images pp. **18** (Archives/The Image Bank), **5** (Kamil Vojnar); Mary Evans Picture Library pp. **10**, **29** (Peter Underwood); Masterfile p. **14** (Nora Good); Pics of Scotland p. **21** (Ashley Coombes); Rex Features p. **22** (Sutton Hibbert JSU); TopFoto pp. **9** (Charles Walker), **25** (Fortean).

Cover image of a Halloween decoration reproduced with permission of Masterfile (Brian Sytnyk).

The publishers would like to thank Diana Bentley, Nancy Harris, and Dee Reid for their assistance in the preparation of this book.

Contents

Some words are printed in bold, **like this**. You can find out what they mean in the glossary. You can also look in the box at the bottom of the page where the word first appears.

What Are Ghosts?

Some people believe that a ghost is the energy of a person that stays on Earth after the person dies. People call this a spirit.

Body and spirit

There are some people who believe that our bodies and our spirits are only connected when we are alive. They believe that when we die, our bodies are buried, but our spirits remain.

There are other people who believe that when the body dies, the spirit dies, too. They do not believe that ghosts exist.

Are ghosts dangerous?

Many people are **petrified** of ghosts. Some have reported that a ghost tried to harm them. But many people who are interested in ghosts believe they are not dangerous.

What do you think?

Do you believe in ghosts?

petrified very scared

Some people say that when a ghost appears, you may suddenly feel hot or cold, or the hairs on the back of your neck might stand up.

Many people have reported going toward a light when they have a near-death experience.

Why Ghosts Are Here

When people come close to dying but survive, they often say that they see a bright light.

Going into the light

Some people think that ghosts occur when the spirit does not understand that it should go into this light. In fact, the spirit may not even realize that the body is dead.

Other people suggest that ghosts may want us to help them figure out what happened to them. Once they understand, they are ready to head to wherever spirits should go. There they may become entities other than ghosts. We do not see them after that.

Spooky fact

Certain people say that ghosts have trouble moving on because they had some unfinished business in their lives.

What Ghosts Look Like

People often say that ghosts look the same as when they were alive, except now they are transparent and misty.

Ghostly fashion

Ghosts may appear in the clothes of their time period. The ghost of a Native American from the 1700s would wear animal skins, while a ghostly **medieval** knight would wear armor.

A number of people say that not only humans become ghosts. People have also reported seeing ghosts of animals.

Ghosts as orbs

However, ghosts may not look like any of this. They may appear as small streaks of light or glowing spots called **orbs**. These orbs zip through the air in unpredictable patterns.

medieval	**from the Middle Ages in Europe, a period that lasted from about C.E. 1000 to 1500**
orb	**object shaped like a ball**
transparent	**see-through**

Spooky story

This is the library of Combermere Abbey. When this photo was taken, Lord Combermere was being buried nearby. The woman who took the photo said that the library had been empty. Can you see anyone?

Spooky fact

Some people think poltergeists are not ghosts, but are people who have telekinesis, the ability to move things without touching them.

Types of Ghost

Certain ghosts may communicate with the living.

Ghostly noises

Ghosts may make sounds to get our attention, or they might even speak. Our ears cannot always hear them, but tape recorders have captured mysterious voices.

Other ghosts do not communicate with people or even notice them. People say these ghosts replay one action over and over, such as walking up stairs. They are more like a recording than a ghost.

Noisy ghosts

Poltergeist is German for "noisy ghost." Poltergeists are unseen, but they may slam a door, move and lift objects, or knock something over.

poltergeist	**type of ghost or force that is not seen, but one that moves things and makes noises**
telekinesis	**ability to move things without touching them**

Unseen Ghosts

"You look like you've seen a ghost," people occasionally say to someone who looks afraid. But not all ghost encounters are sightings.

Ways to sense a ghost

Parapsychologists, or people who study the **supernatural**, claim that many ghost encounters do not involve our vision. Instead people may hear footsteps when no one is around to make them. They may have a feeling that someone is watching them, or they may smell a type of cologne or perfume that no one in the room is wearing.

Spooky fact

In a university music hall in Washington State, the organ sometimes plays when no one is sitting at it.

parapsychologist	**person who studies ghosts or other supernatural situations**
supernatural	**different from understood rules of nature**

People often report hearing, feeling, or even smelling what could be a ghost.

Ghosts tend to stay in one location. People then say that place is haunted.

behead cut off someone's head

Where People Encounter Ghosts

Ghost sightings often happen in a location that meant something to the ghosts when they were alive. It is not always their home. They might show up at a school they attended or hang out at their favorite restaurant.

Ghosts are everywhere

Many reports say that battlefields are major ghost sites, because many people died there. Theaters are another popular spot for ghosts, because ghosts are drawn to emotions, and people often laugh or cry during a play. Some haunted hotels keep quiet about their ghostly guests because they do not want to frighten their living guests away.

Spooky fact

In the past, prisoners were beheaded at the Tower of London. Visitors today say they often see a female ghost holding her own head.

GHOST TOWNS

Ghost towns are communities that people have abandoned. They exist around the world and were often once mining towns. When all the metal was mined, the people left, but the buildings stayed.

Woman in the windows

Did anything else stay? Some ghost towns are believed to be haunted. St. Elmo, Colorado, was founded in 1878. Soon 2,000 people lived there, but by 1930, only seven people remained in the crumbling town.

One person who stayed was Annabelle Stark. She lived most of her life in St. Elmo and died there in 1960. Since then people say they have seen a woman in a white dress in the windows of the empty old hotel. Some people say that Annabelle's ghost is watching over the town that died before she did.

abandon leave something or someone behind on purpose

Many ghost towns are in the western part of the United States.

What do you think?

Do you think the woman in the white dress could be Annabelle's ghost?

A human cannot usually force out a ghost.

Living With Ghosts

Certain individuals may not mind sharing space with a ghost. Others want the ghost to move out immediately, or else they will.

Problem ghosts

Some ghosts may not be scary, while other ghosts that people report are annoying more than anything else.

Some people call a ghost hunter to see if they really do have a ghost. Others try to communicate with their ghost housemate, perhaps asking the ghost to leave. If the ghost stays, the people may even get used to its company. Either way it is the ghost's decision.

What do you think?

What would you do if you thought a ghost was living in your house?

Ghost Hunters

Ghost hunters are not ghostbusters. They do not fight ghosts, and they do not expel unwanted ghosts from people's houses.

How ghost hunters work

The **mission** of a ghost hunter is to use science to prove that ghosts exist. Ghost hunters know that stories are not enough to convince most people. They try to get **evidence**, such as photographs, video, and audio recordings.

Many ghost hunters do not make much, or any, money from ghost hunting. They do it because they are fascinated by the **supernatural**.

Spooky fact

Ghost hunters often work at night, so they need equipment such as night vision goggles and a motion detector. These things help them to work in the dark.

evidence	**facts**
mission	**purpose for doing something**

Ghost hunters want to help the living understand what ghosts are and what they might want.

motion detector	**machine used to signal when something moves nearby**
night vision goggles	**eyewear used to see in the dark**

This $100 ghost radar can pick up magnetic interference and other supernatural rays.

atmosphere	air that surrounds Earth
electromagnetic energy	type of energy made of electrical and magnetic waves
infrasound	noise that is too low for humans to hear
sound wave	how sound moves through the air

The Science of Ghosts

No one has ever captured and studied a ghost. However, some people think ghosts might be made from electromagnetic energy. This energy is always in the atmosphere.

Feeling sounds

To find out what ghosts are, scientists need to rule out what ghosts are *not*. Some people think they feel a ghost when what they really feel is **infrasound**. This is a **sound wave** that is too low for humans to hear. However, we can sense its vibration, which may send chills down our spine.

Spooky fact

Ghost hunters use instruments to check how much electromagnetic energy is in the air. If the level is high, a ghost might be causing it.

Famous Ghosts

Some ghosts become famous. Some famous people also become ghosts.

The Brown Lady

The Brown Lady of Raynham Hall in England is a famous ghost. She may be the ghost of a woman who died in 1726. Witnesses say the ghost wears a brown dress and has empty holes for eyes.

In 1936 two magazine photographers were at Raynham Hall. One saw the ghost coming down a large staircase. The other saw nothing, but snapped a now-famous picture in that direction.

Spooky story

Abraham Lincoln may still be in the White House, as a ghost. Several people have seen him, from President Calvin Coolidge's wife to former British Prime Minister Winston Churchill.

Numerous people think this 1936 photo of the Brown Lady is the best ghost photo ever taken.

The ghosts in *A Christmas Carol* visit Scrooge on Christmas Eve.

Fictional Ghosts

People love a good ghost story.

Ghosts in print

The book *A Christmas Carol* by Charles Dickens was first published in 1843. It is a story about three ghosts who visit an uncharitable man named Scrooge. The ghosts want to scare Scrooge into being a kinder and more generous person.

Another kind of ghost first appeared in 1945: *Casper the Friendly Ghost*. Casper has starred in cartoons and comic books ever since.

Ghosts on screen

The 1984 comedy movie *Ghostbusters* was about people who are hired to capture ghosts. Many other movies have been made about ghosts, and many of them are spooky.

What do you think?

Why do you think ghost stories are so popular?

Are Ghosts Real?

For centuries people in many cultures have searched for the truth about ghosts.

What we do not know

There are many opinions about what happens to us when we die.

Does everyone become a ghost? Or just some people? Or no one? We do not know.

If ghosts do exist, we do not know where they "live." They may live in our world, or they may live in another **dimension**. If they do, they may be able to visit our world whenever they want. Perhaps some get trapped in our world.

What we do know

The strange lights, noises, and feelings that people report are real. One day we may learn if ghosts are causing them.

dimension unseen place where things exist at the same time that we do

What do you think?

So do you think ghosts exist?

Some people believe in ghosts even though they have never seen one.

Glossary

abandon leave something or someone behind on purpose

atmosphere air that surrounds Earth

behead cut off someone's head

dimension unseen place where things exist at the same time that we do

electromagnetic energy type of energy made of electrical and magnetic waves

evidence facts

infrasound noise that is too low for humans to hear

medieval from the Middle Ages in Europe, a period that lasted from about C.E. 1000 to 1500

mission purpose for doing something

motion detector machine used to signal when something moves nearby

night vision goggles eyewear used to see in the dark

orb object shaped like a ball

parapsychologist person who studies ghosts or other supernatural situations

petrified very scared

poltergeist type of ghost or force that is not seen, but one that moves things and makes noises

sound wave how sound moves through the air

supernatural different from understood rules of nature

telekinesis ability to move things without touching them

transparent see-through

Want to know more?

Books

* Brucken, Kelli M. *Ghosts (Mysterious Encounters)*. San Diego: Kidhaven Press, 2006.
* Farman, John. *The Short and Bloody History of Ghosts*. Minneapolis: Lerner, 2002.
* Watkins, Graham. *Ghosts and Poltergeists*. New York: Rosen, 2002.

If you liked this Atomic book, why don't you try these...?

Index